DELTA

DELTA

BRIDGE OVER TROUBLED DREAMS

The emotional stories behind Delta Goodrem's
sixth studio album.

**SIMON &
SCHUSTER**

London · New York · Sydney · Toronto · New Delhi

BRIDGE OVER TROUBLED DREAMS
First published in Australia in 2021 by Simon & Schuster (Australia) Pty Limited
Suite 19A, Level 1, Building C, 450 Miller Street, Cammeray, NSW 2062

10 9 8 7 6 5 4 3

Sydney New York London Toronto New Delhi

Visit our website at www.simonandschuster.com.au

 A catalogue record for this
book is available from the
National Library of Australia

ISBN: 9781761101298

Cover and internal design: Meng Koach
Cover image: Carlotta Moye
Internal and endpaper images courtesy: Carlotta Moye, Ashleigh Larden,
Matthew Copley, Joseph Dadic, Marla Altschuler and Delta Goodrem

Every effort has been made to acknowledge and contact the copyright holders for permission
to reproduce material contained in this book. Any copyright holders who have been
inadvertently omitted from acknowledgements and credits should contact the publisher
and omissions will be rectified in subsequent editions.

Printed and bound in Great Britain by Bell and Bain Ltd, Glasgow

To my family, my friends, my ride-or-dies, the passing ships in my life;
to all who have left fingerprints on my heart, my gratitude for you
knows no bounds.

To you who is reading this book, thank you for taking me into your home
and your heart, without even realising the impact you have had on me
and how you touched my life. You will never know how much a simple
smile or a barista saying 'Hi Delta' means to me. Growing up in front
of you, making mistakes in front of you, learning in front of you is
a privilege and an honour. We have been in this relationship together
for a while and now it's time to get deeper.

My mum once said she was sad her parents passed away before they
had the chance to share in my journey and I told her not to worry —
I have an entire nation of aunties, uncles, grandmas, grandpas, sisters
and brothers, all of whom I count as a part of this story.

This one's for you.

Award-winning Australian singer, songwriter and actress Delta Goodrem has been inspiring the world with her music since she signed her first record deal with Sony Music Australia at the age of 15. The internationally acclaimed, multi-platinum artist has spent much of her time in the US and UK over the past two decades, dedicating herself to her craft and creating an unrivalled body of work – but at the end of the day, she still calls Australia home.

Over the years, Delta has accrued nine No. 1 singles, four No. 1 albums, 17 top-10 hits, 12 ARIA Awards, a Silver Logie Award and three World Music Awards – not to mention amassing a dedicated fan base around the world. Her first studio offering, *Innocent Eyes*, was one of the highest-selling debut albums in Australian history, spending a record-breaking 29 weeks at No. 1, topping the Australian Albums Charts and achieving 23-times platinum sales. Since then, Delta has gone from strength to strength, releasing hit records, selling out arena shows and showcasing her incredible artistry on both stage and screen.

The talented multi-hyphenate is now adding yet another string to her bow with her first book, *Bridge Over Troubled Dreams,* sharing a rare, intimate glimpse inside the process behind her sixth studio album (of the same name) and how each track was brought to life.

Contents

Introduction   10

Keep Climbing   18

Everyone's Famous   28

Solid Gold   40

Dear Elton   52

Behind The Scenes   62

Billionaire   70

Paralyzed   78

All Of My Friends   90

Kill Them With Kindness   98

Crash   108

Play   116

Album Credits   128

INTRODUCTION

In October 2018, I faced one of the biggest challenges of my life. After having surgery to remove a salivary gland, I woke up to discover that I could no longer control my speech.

Complications during the operation had left a nerve in my tongue paralysed. When a nerve is damaged this way, it has to be taught to communicate with its receptors again and that process is completely unforgiving. I was told that the damaged nerve would likely heal naturally in its own time, but the doctors couldn't predict how my recovery would look. They said it could take three months, a year, three years before I learnt to speak and sing as I once could... or it may not happen at all.

My sound is my livelihood and I was facing losing that altogether.

But I'm nothing if not a fighter, and I saw this chapter of my life for what it was: a rebirth. This was my time to be silent and to observe. It was not my time to speak; it was my time to listen and to hear everything else that was going on in the world.

And so began The Reset.

STOP & REWIND

After 'TongueGate', as I call it, I met with a few different people to start writing music, but when you're put into a room with someone you've never met before to make something as deeply personal as I wanted this record to be, it's a little bit like an arranged marriage. The creatives I was working with were incredibly talented, but I found it hard to go deeper with them as quickly as I needed to.

So two of my amazing team members sat me down at the table in my place in LA, opened Voice Memos on their phones and we began talking about my life. We started from the very beginning – quite literally, with the story of my birth, which itself became a song – and we talked and talked like this for four days, morning to night. These two women, two of my most trusted kindred spirits in the world, asked me questions and helped me dive deeper than I ever had before, peeling back the layers of my history and helping me discover that I have nothing to hide. As we reached the end of this intense purge days later, I suddenly realised: 'So that's how I got here.'

It was incredible.

After that, the writing just flowed. We pulled themes from my life, some of which came up again and again, and then I tapped into my inspiration, sat at my piano and started playing the sounds of my life. All of my

> *'This chapter is about truth. It's about me being transparent, saying things out loud that I've always held inside. It's about who I am and who I have always been deep down'*

albums so far have been about a chapter in time, but every song on *Bridge Over Troubled Dreams* is a single page pulled from each of those chapters. It shares my stories of lessons learnt, love, family, highs and lows, patience, freedom, faith, hope and survival, and times when failure has been my reward.

I still have days when I get a little frustrated with my tongue, when I feel it's not as easy to sing, but that's just a work in progress. And even in those moments, I do always recognise that I am healthy, I have a great roof over my head, I have family and friends... I'm truly so lucky and not everybody is. Everyone has a story, everyone has their own challenges that are unique to them and while I do feel I attract extremes sometimes – my stories can be quite dramatic! – I definitely consider myself so fortunate.

I'm someone who has lived a few lifetimes by a young age, but because of that I can go deeper and connect on another level with those who have also faced challenges and struggles. The more you experience, the more the colours in your internal rainbow – things like compassion, understanding, openness – begin to deepen. I feel like I have a better understanding of what people are going through because I've also been through similar moments – and that is a gift.

FROM THESE HAMMERS, STRINGS & WOOD

In my teens, it looked like I was following the playbook to the letter. I took each step in the order that was expected of me to build my dream career. I stepped

through every door as it opened and I always tried to bring my best to everything I did. Did I nail it straight away? Maybe, maybe not; and maybe there is no 'right' way to do things. But I know I work hard enough to get it right the second time around.

Dreams don't have an expiry date and that's been a really important lesson for me. That's why it's such a prominent theme on the album. When you're in your twenties, your early twenties in particular, there's a mixture of invincibility and excitement as you embark on adulthood, but there's an innocence underlying it

love you girl ♡
Olive ♡ xx

all, too. What I wanted to portray through this record is the view from the next level; from the perspective of having lived it and breathed it. I want to make 20-year-olds excited about turning 30!

I poured my life story into these lyrics and I needed the sound to match the realness and intensity of the words. Each song represents a different moment from my life and, as such, is unique, but the overall sound is distinct, weaving every track together in a musical tapestry. I wanted it to have an edge to it, a cool-chic factor that sets it apart. If Elton John and Adele had

a baby, I would want it to be this album. One can dream, right?!

I wrote every single song at the piano, stripping my sound back to basics. In the same way that Elton's piano drives the energy and pace of his songs, so do the keys define and power this record – though choirs, counter melodies, '60s electric guitar, live instruments and orchestral strings add layers of texture and depth. I also love harmonies – I'm a harmony junkie! – and that comes through in *Bridge Over Troubled Dreams*. I purposely steered clear of electric keys and overproduced beats on this album – I wanted it to be real, raw, fresh and modern, with each sound carefully chosen for its meaning and purpose.

The piano holds a special place both on this record and in my heart, and there are so many who inspire the way I play on these tracks. The way Coldplay pair the keys with their use of strings is iconic. They find simple, repeated patterns that quickly become earworms. I think many who play piano look to the band's front man, Chris Martin, as a master because he has his own unique style. His records have had an ability to tap into my curiosity about the world and my adventurous spirit. Elton John wouldn't be Elton John without his trademark piano sound, either; the sound of Joe Cocker's piano inspires a very distinct throwback feeling. Lady Gaga live is something else – she feels strong and powerful when she performs, as if she's riding a galloping horse on stage. There are beautiful eccentricities in Tori Amos' musical choices as her fingers seemingly dance along the piano keys in ways you couldn't imagine. All these artists have this in common: they are free.

There's a cool factor to the songs on *Bridge Over Troubled Dreams* that I hadn't yet explored in my career. I leaned into all the elements that make me the artist I am today: my huskiness, my quirky side, my classical piano influences and a toughness that I haven't brought to my previous records. Sprinkled on top is what Einstein might've called a 'spooky' factor – that certain something that you can't quite explain. I think mine lies in my eccentricity and authenticity.

THE BRUSCHETTA THEORY

Confession: I can't cook. But my partner Matthew definitely can. He makes an incredible bruschetta and getting it right, he says, is all about using the best ingredients. He chooses the freshest bread to be the base of the dish; a perfectly firm, bright red, ripe tomato; vibrant green basil; top-shelf olive oil... there are only five or six elements, but each one is carefully and lovingly chosen to ensure the end result is a masterpiece.

This became my own personal theory as I began work on this record: the Bruschetta Theory. Simple key ingredients of the highest quality, all working together in harmony to create a masterpiece.

With this in mind, I began a search for the best 'piece of bread' – which, for my music, is the piano. Instead of just going to a studio and accepting what they had, I went to loads of different studios and tested their pianos until I found the right one. It's something I had never done in my career, because I'd always just felt that I had to make do with what was available and adapt my style to suit the piano. But my thumbprint on music, the thing that draws it all together, has always been my style of playing. I'm quite random, quite spontaneous and I don't adhere much to structure.

As a player, I'm a composer. The way I play is the way I feel in that moment, so having a connection to the instrument I'm using is key to delivering a sound that is genuinely me. Some of the pianos I tried sounded too old, some were too fresh, some were too bright... And, honestly, it was the most amazing experience! I feel like I learnt more about production while creating this record than I have in 10 years.

In fact, stepping back to before the work began on this record, a similar metaphor could be applied to the various musos who intrigued me most while writing these songs. These artists tapped into different parts of me and I mixed those elements together the way a chef would combine different spices in just the right quantities to come up with a delicious and unique final dish. Vocally, Jeff Buckley became an interesting and awesome reference for me. There is a certain mystery to his sound that stabs right into the heart of his songs. I love the mathematics of Bishop Briggs' production, and while she's a little more aggressive than I am, the simplicity of what she does hits me hard: it's edgy lyrics paired with rougher moments on top of pulsing, moody chords. The way Adele's voice soars touches my soul, and Annie Lennox's ad-libbing conveys a statement and a feeling without ever taking away from the melody. I love Emeli Sandé's vocal chains, Lewis Capaldi's husky sound, Hozier's intensity... These are the artists whose voices make me lean in. I could go on and on – I've been a student of music from the day I started and I love dissecting this craft. I have created and kept scrapbooks of every single record I've made, filled with inspiration, from imagery to sounds (as I've mentioned), words and anything else that sparks that fire within. This book is my way of sharing one of these scrapbooks – my 'adult' book for an 'adult' record.

THE SOUND OF LIFE

The art of an album is one of the closest sensory experiences we have to a real-life time machine. Electricity sparks as each note is brought to life by the emotion in a singer's tone; this conveys the story and together they produce a sound that completely embodies the feeling you're experiencing. The music and the lyrics wrap around you and leave an imprint on your soul, and when you hear it again in a different chapter of your life, you're instantly transported to that space and time.

'The world is loving transparency right now; people are craving talent amongst the noise of the posers — and it's very loud out there'

There are musicians you connect to in fleeting moments and then there are artists who become part of your life's soundtrack. For example, Coldplay is one of those for me. They've always had an ability to create music that had a fantastical side and an ethereal nature but with the grounding of a 100-year-old tree, with wisdom and depth. They perfectly intertwine real instruments and conversational lyrics with enough mystery to allow me to see my own life experiences play out in their songs. I was recently asked to write a love letter to a record and I chose Coldplay's sixth studio album, *Ghost Stories*. This album calmed me in a time when I was surrounded by chaos. It gave me

a sparkle of hope with a touch of melancholy that really spoke to me. This album allowed my heart to bleed while also slowly and gently stitching it back up again. My soul's open wounds were able to heal while I listened to the music – which I did everywhere, from start to finish, time and again. I would stare at the sky and listen for hours, the songs giving me a gentle kick to try to move forward, but also allowing me to hold space for how I felt. So when I'm making an album, these are the traits I remember as an observer.

My appreciation and gratitude for the artists who inspire me and set my soul on fire can bring me to

tears. They have been there for me as a lifelong source of inspiration and a safe place where I can sit and just be myself. Being a fellow 'piano dancer', I would count myself as someone who can hold their own in most scenarios. But I have to admit, my passion for these artists has led to some uncomfortable face-to-face meetings! Chris Martin, for example – every time he and I have met in person, I have been super awkward, said something vastly uncool, wildly embarrassed myself and then spent the next hour with my head in the palm of my hands thinking about whatever weird thing I said!

I have this same awe-inspired awkwardness around a handful of other artists. Elton John is one. Olivia Newton-John – it took me years to be a normal human being in front of Olivia! She's one of my dearest friends now but before we knew each other well, she would call me all the time and I just didn't know how to act around her. And I still remember embarrassing myself when I met Daniel Johns for the first time, too,

'I'm in this for the long haul, I always have been. It's a marathon, not a sprint'

more than 20 years ago! I was 14, at the ARIA Awards, and Daniel commented on how bright my dress was (it was a hot pink number I'd had specially made). I started rambling, as I've always done when I'm nervous, telling him, 'Oh yes, my mum says you could probably see it from space and the fabric is waterproof, so I could go swimming in it if I wanted to...' I still remember the look on his face afterwards. To my mind, I was just talking candidly about my new dress but when I stopped talking, the silence was deafening – I could basically hear the crickets.

These people in my field that I admire so much, who have been so integral to my musical upbringing and development as an artist, who have inspired and influenced me so profoundly to be who I am today – they're the ones who leave me lost for words (or babbling nonsensical ones!).

With all of that said, however, *Bridge Over Troubled Dreams* is unapologetically me. As I wrote, I distanced myself from any expectations of what and who I should be at this point in my career. Writing song after song at the piano with no production to hide behind forced me to go back to my roots and unravel things that I've been holding onto for years. I had the freedom to be within my own thoughts and I don't think I've ever felt as alive as I did while creating this body of work. This is my first 'adult' record and it marks a return to my true best self. It's my 'woman' record; the one to make people say, 'I didn't know she could do that – as a producer and an artist!'

I've gone back to the start of who I am as an artist. I wrote everything at the piano, pushing through chords to uncover who I am now. That's really what this process has been about and as I listen back to all these songs, I feel that I was able to open up with a very different kind of honesty. There's freedom in this music that I haven't felt for a while and it was only after facing the challenge of learning to speak again that I was able to strip away all the frills, all the pieces that no longer felt like me. When I surrendered to that sense of starting over, I began to walk a new path.

KEEP CLIMBING

KEEP CLIMBING

Packed my bags and I walk on foot
This was the time that I knew I should
There's a fear in every step
And I still love where I just left

Two mountains
I'm caught in the middle
Can't see the forest
Before the trees
This climb it
Breaks me a little
But the hope inside of me
That this lonely valley leads
To a bridge over troubled dreams
To a bridge over troubled dreams

I see new lines across my face
And I lost some strength that I can't replace
Am I too tired for this healing?
And are my scars now too revealing?

There's two mountains
I'm caught in the middle
Can't see the forest
Before the trees
This climb it
Breaks me a little
But the hope inside of me
That this lonely valley leads
To a bridge over troubled dreams

Keep climbing
Just keep climbing
Keep climbing
Just keep climbing

Keep climbing
Just keep climbing
Keep climbing
Just keep climbing

Keep climbing
Just keep climbing
Keep climbing
Just keep climbing

Keep climbing
Just keep climbing
Keep climbing

Two mountains
I'm caught in the middle
Can't see the forest
Before the trees
This climb it
Breaks me a little
That this lonely valley leads
To a bridge over troubled dreams

Keep climbing
Just keep climbing
Keep climbing
To a bridge over troubled dreams
Just keep climbing
Keep climbing
Just keep climbing

(Keep climbing)
(Keep climbing)

'I learnt young that change is inevitable. It's always going to happen and that's a good thing'

My home in LA is in a wonderful little complex that's nestled between two mountains and it's in that apartment that I wrote this whole record. But as much as I love it there, I found being tucked away in that valley became something of a metaphor for how I was feeling: caught between where I was going and where I had already been.

As I sat there between these defining life stages and the two mountains, I really felt into that in-between space. Everything I'd already done was on one side of me; everything I wanted to do next lay ahead, and that's what this song is about: recognising both the joys and the setbacks I've been through as well as the challenges and triumphs still to come. I'd already conquered one mountain and as I took stock, reassessed and thought about what was coming next, I realised I had no choice but to climb again. No dreams, however big or small, come without challenges and mine are no exception. We all have to keep moving forward and embrace changes as they come because life is constantly shifting – and that's not a bad thing, which is something I learnt early on.

When I was 18 and battling Hodgkin's lymphoma, a lot of people reached out to me, but one particular note I was sent really stuck with me. It was from Osher Günsberg (he went by Andrew G back then), who wrote, 'This change is a good change, like all changes are.' Those words always run through my mind when things are evolving around me. I've always been somebody who adapts quickly to change, perhaps because I've had so many starts and stops along the way. I will feel into the gravity of the situation, but it's never long before I'm saying to myself, 'Okay, this has happened and now it's time to move forward.' I've learnt how to constantly redefine myself throughout the industry's ever-changing seasons and stay at the top of my game.

'I needed to be okay with having troubled dreams, as dreaming was the only way I could get to the other side of the mountain'

Another shift happened for me as I approached my mid-thirties, around the time I wrote this track. For me (and several of my girlfriends, too), turning 35 brought with it a reassessment of life. Obviously we're still young! But I was questioning everything I'd done up until that point. I was definitely feeling comfortable in my skin, but I was also looking back at my career and thinking: 'Did I get it right? Am I doing okay? Is this what I wanted? Is it where I want to be? Is this where I'm going?' Questions like those can be pretty confronting.

I first appeared on TV when I was seven and I had a normal childhood. But by 16, I was living life in the public eye. I made some really great moves, but I also made some interesting ones along the way. If I had known then what I know now, would I have

made different decisions, walked different paths? Of course there's no way to know the answer to that, but the more I thought it over, the more I was inspired by the idea that failures are not really failures. Rather, they're experiences and instead of regretting anything from our past, we should use change to learn and grow. Every choice I have made has made me who I am – and I really like who I am.

In spite of the questions and the uncertainty, I'm also filled with so much hope right now and that's reflected in this track, too. To keep climbing means never giving up. Life is messy, being a human is messy; but it's so important to keep going and continue to face what life throws at you as you make your way to your dreams.

EVERYONE'S FAMOUS

EVERYONE'S FAMOUS

You want to be famous
And fly for your life to the stars
Not think twice who you are
Just use what your mama gave
Do you think you can take it?
Love it or hate it
Is this worth the world to you right now?
Give up your family, your blood, the crowd

Oh you think this is easy
That dreaming comes cheaply
Are you ready to dance with the devil and sell
Your soul and you think — well I might as well

Superstars in the sky
Passing by
Stumbling in the dark
I wonder why
And I've tried — I'm not high
Everyone's famous tonight

I thought it had meaning
When I grew up dreaming
Watching Mariah and Whitney and Cher
Kill it on stage was an art that we praised

Oh forget about greatness
'Cause everyone's famous
If that's what you want
Then I wish that I'd known
And just sung my songs here on my own

Superstars in the sky
Passing by
Stumbling in the dark
I wonder why
And I've tried — I'm not high
Everyone's famous

I'll let you in on a secret
But it comes and it goes
But if you really are a star
You'll always be...

A superstar in the sky
Passing by
Stumbling in the dark
I wonder why
And I've I tried
Is everyone famous tonight?

Superstars in the sky
Passing by
Stumbling in the dark
I wonder why
And I've tried — I'm not high
Everyone's famous tonight

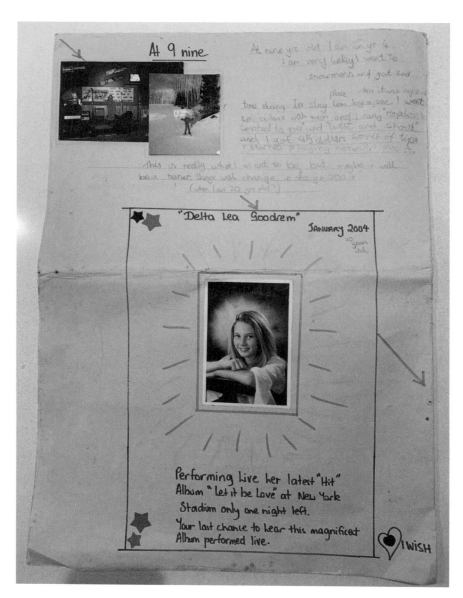

At 9 nine

At nine yrs old I am in yr 4
I am very lucky I went to
snowmass and got 2nd
place — the it was my 2nd
time skiing. In stay teen by a sec I went
to a bar with mum and I sang "Hopeless
devoted to you" and "twist and shout"
and I got 45 dollars worth of tips
I started playing netball — love it.

This is really what I want to be, but maybe it will
be a runner things will change in the year 2004
(when I am 70 yrs old?)

"Delta Lea Goodrem"   January 2004
                            70 years old

Performing live her latest "Hit"
Album "Let it be Love" at New York
Stadium only one night left.
Your last chance to hear this magnificent
Album performed live.

I WISH

PREDICT YOUR FUTURE

'Being a superstar is about heart and soul and hard work'

Growing up these days is so different from when I was a kid. I wanted to reach for the stars, be like the legends; I was obsessed with learning the craft. But thanks to social media, fame is so accessible now that it's taken on a different meaning. *Everyone's Famous* is an observation on society and how popularity – and the means of achieving it – has shifted.

It's not uncommon to hear kids say they want to be 'famous' when they grow up, but they don't necessarily talk about what fuels that desire. With Instagram, YouTube and other social media outlets, it's more possible than ever to become a celebrity, and there's absolutely nothing wrong with that – in fact, I always had this vision of bringing a kids' choir in to sing the line '*superstars in the sky, passing by*' to give the song that sense of innocence. But when I was young and I'd say I wanted to be like Mariah Carey or Whitney Houston or Cher – the greats – I wasn't talking about their star status. It didn't ever enter my brain to simply say I wanted to be famous, because it was about the art of music, it was about being outstanding in my field, about my passion for the craft. For me, celebrity was (and still is, really) the by-product of being somebody who is so passionate about music and connection and storytelling. The rest of it was never a striving point for me.

It's probably no surprise that I don't use the term celebrity to describe myself; I don't say I'm famous and I've never responded well when people refer to me that way. Yes, I grew up in the public eye, but fame isn't what I do and it's actually uncomfortable for me to think of myself in that way. I'm an artist, a muso – and when it comes to being in the spotlight, I just try to do my very best to be a good role model and create a safe space for everyone.

There's no denying that there has been an immense culture and energy shift. When I released *Innocent Eyes* at 18, iPhones didn't exist; iTunes was only just coming into play. If you wanted access to music, you went to the shop and you bought an album or a single on CD, or – going back even further – lined up a cassette tape and hit record when your favourite song came on the radio! But the ever-changing landscape of celebrity today makes me a little concerned for the next generation who are coming up and whether they realise what fame really entails.

'We are truly all just
learning as we go'

35

'Having kids sing on this track means so much to me; it's as if I'm talking to a child version of myself'

Reality TV, for example. I love it, don't get me wrong. I sit and binge watch on the couch with my friends just like everyone else! But what I would say to people when they get onto these shows and find themselves suddenly thrust into the spotlight is to remember all that comes with it. So much can be brought to light that people wouldn't expect and when those deeply personal moments are exposed, I genuinely worry and wonder if they'll be okay dealing with such intimate details being made public.

So in that way, *Everyone's Famous* is also a bit of a warning. As the lyric says, '*you think this is easy, the dreaming comes cheaply*' but when people have their sights set on stardom, they can be blind to some of those more destructive downsides. I find that I can deal with the harder aspects of being in the public eye because it comes as a result of my love for creating music and TV, and my care for and genuine connection with people. My constant focus is always, *always* on my craft. I think it would be so hard to experience celebrity without having a drive or a passion underlying it.

Fame also has the ability to change you. I've watched it happen to people around me and I've learnt in my career that if someone is going to change, it will likely happen pretty quickly. I've seen the humblest hopefuls on *The Voice* start their journey gracious and grateful, and within a couple of performances their attitude completely flips. I've also noticed that the common factor amongst those who stay grounded seems to be their dedication to the music, rather than the desire for celebrity status.

'I'm not so much a love writer as a life observer...'

Everyone's Famous is also an ode to some of the greats. I wanted to share my gratitude and admiration for those who influenced me during my childhood and who continue to do so today – and that isn't limited to musicians. I loved basketball growing up so the Netflix show *The Last Dance*, about Michael Jordan's career, was incredible to me. He was famous for his talent and the greatness he strove for. They inspired me to always aim high, and I wonder sometimes if that passion, that drive for success – no matter the industry you're in or the life you are living – has been forgotten in people's search for large-scale recognition.

The fact that the world's changed is a good thing, I really believe that and I would never discourage anyone from putting themselves out there and creating whatever life they choose – more power to them! I think that's amazing and they should be applauded. Just don't let it stop the process of striving for true greatness – and that's at the heart of this track: in the search for fame, put passion first.

There's another aspect to this song, though, that is so important to note. The bridge says, '*I'll let you in on a secret... that if you really are a star, you'll always be a superstar, in the sky, passing by...*' Meaning, if you do have a calling, listen to that voice inside telling you to go for it. The lyric that says we're all '*stumbling in the dark*' is also brutally honest – none of us really know where we're going and nobody is perfect. But let's not forget about the value of hard work and grounding yourself in doing what you're called to do. As long as we keep aiming for the stars, any dream is possible.

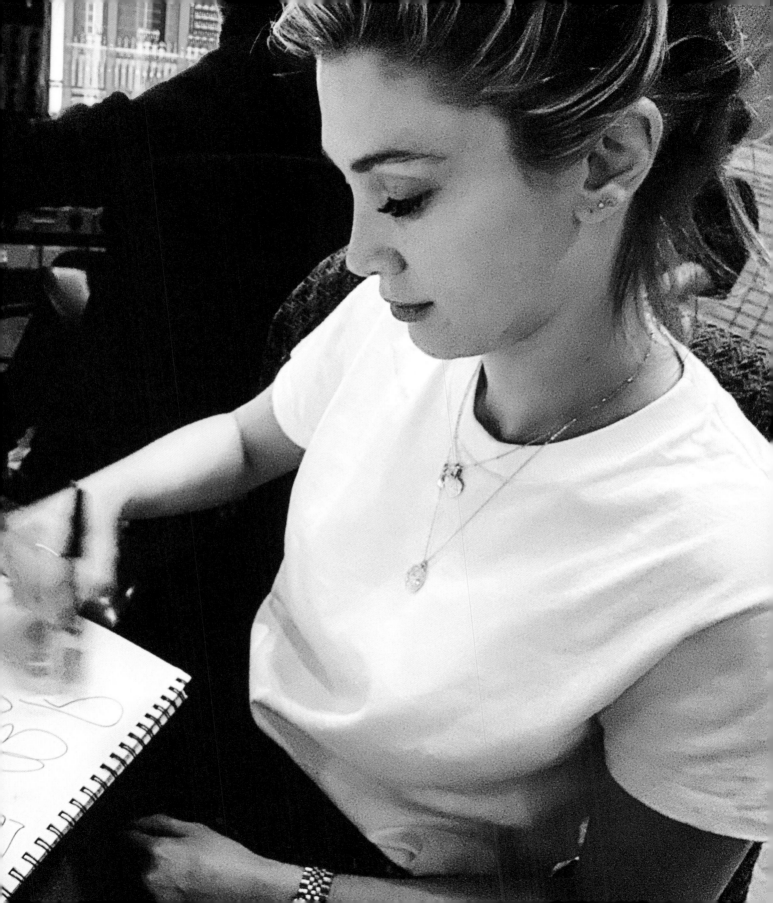

SOLID GOLD

SOLID GOLD

You whisper, 'I love you'
Then I feel the wind as you run out the door
It's only now I see the pattern
You push the limit of my heart
I can't keep up when you're dragging me down
Take it or leave my skin and bones, ohhh

I wake up from the storm
To my world on the floor
And I'm crying
From the times that you stood in my way

I'm going to take your bad heart
And turn it into a small dot
It's gonna turn to coal
And then I'll burn it all
And all of these embers
Are gonna make you remember
That what you had
Was always solid gold

Have I been sleeping with disaster?
You can't un-kiss the damage you've done
I know this sign it's a heavy warning, ohhh

I wake up from the storm
I got nothing to lose
Like the rain swept the weight from my chest

I'm going to take your bad heart
And turn it into a small dot
It's gonna turn to coal
And then I'll burn it all
And all of these embers
Are gonna make you remember
That what you had
Was always solid gold
Was always solid gold

You whisper, 'I love you'
To no-one 'cause I'm already gone
You pushed the limit of my love

I'm going to take your bad heart
And turn it into a small dot
It's gonna turn to coal
And then I'll burn it all, yeah
And all of these embers
Are gonna make you remember
That what you had
Was always solid gold
Was always solid gold

Every record needs an empowering 'hell, yes!' song and that's what *Solid Gold* is! I wrote it in the studio with Matt and another team member, Marla – who is brilliant, by the way, and I believe in her genius. They were jamming on the guitar and I went running in when I heard them hit on something truly special. I just started singing that verse melody and the whole thing evolved really organically.

The track is about finding your inner strength and listening to your intuition; it's about finding the courage to walk away from things that no longer serve you. These could be romantic relationships, business partnerships, toxic friendships... any scenario where you've been left

'Pressure makes diamonds...'

questioning your self-worth. And it's not only about knowing that you'll be just fine without them but also realising that you can learn and grow from that experience; you can take everything you've learnt and do something positive with it. You can turn those situations into solid gold.

It's not a revenge song by any means. It's a celebration of courage and a recognition of your own strength and inner beauty. It's about rising above and knowing your own value. I always enter every situation with an open heart. I lead with love but if you can't take in what I'm sending out, I'll put that energy into something and someone else who can.

Leaving behind the people and scenarios that don't serve me hasn't always come easy, though; it is definitely something I've had to learn along the way. I'm incredibly loyal when people are good to me but that trait has, on occasion, been to my detriment. When I was younger, I stayed too long in certain situations out of a misplaced sense of indebtedness. I used to see the potential in people; I saw who they

'Letting go of the things that no longer serve us isn't always easy'

could be, rather than seeing them for who they were at the time. But I did learn that lesson and *Solid Gold* speaks to that: standing up for yourself, knowing what you bring to the table and being comfortable walking away when you're being undervalued.

Being able to put situations into perspective was also key to this growth for me and a dear friend of mine demonstrated the concept so perfectly at a time when I was feeling incredibly overwhelmed. He held up a piece of paper and told me to poke a hole through

47

it with my finger. I did, and he said to me, 'If you look at the entire piece of paper, it seems too big to deal with. But if you focus on that one tiny hole, that small dot, you take back control and it becomes manageable.' That's the idea behind the lyric, '*I'm going to take your bad heart and turn it into a small dot*' – I won't let things get any bigger than they have to be; I won't be engulfed by what seems like the enormity of those negative emotions.

There have been numerous times in my career when I've had to be brave and stand up for my worth and, honestly, they're my proudest moments. In those times when I've been devalued – whether it's because I'm the only Australian in the room or because

I'm a woman, or for some other reason – I have stepped back, become the quiet observer and thought, 'I still know my worth; I know what I bring. I will always show up on time and be my very best. I know I can load the bases and I know I can hit the home run.' Those things can be hard to remember when people are tearing you down – but how you handle adversity shines a light on your character and shapes you for the future.

As the saying goes, pressure makes diamonds – or, in the metaphor of this song, gold. No matter what life throws at you, you are solid gold. Know your worth and you'll have the strength to walk away with your head held high.

'There are still moments when I need to remind myself to stand strong and remember my worth'

DEAR ELTON

DEAR ELTON

I guess it didn't go the way I thought it would
You did your part and I lost mine
I was so young and chose the hard way
It isn't an excuse to be a freight train

What do I got to do with this connection?
When I feel it in my heart
Even when we're worlds apart

Have I let you down, Rocket Man?
I haven't been around, but here I am
You have given songs to everyone
And now this song's from me
Piano Man, do you understand?
Here I am

I guess that I have finally arrived now
I feel like I am truly my own self
And maybe the crowd got tired and went home
I wouldn't blame anyone, it's my own

What do I got to do with this connection?
When I feel it in my heart
Even when we're worlds apart

Have I let you down, Rocket Man?
I haven't been around, but here I am
You have given songs to everyone
Now this song's from me
Piano Man, do you understand?
Here I am
Here I am

What do I got to do with this connection?
When I feel it in my heart
Even when we're worlds apart

Have I let you down, Rocket Man?
I haven't been around, but here I am
You have given songs to everyone
And now this song's from me
Piano Man, do you understand?
Here I am
Here I am

This song is a letter to Elton John and in many
ways I don't even know how it happened.
I was completely lost inside the music while
I was writing, pounding and pounding on the keys,
so desperate to tell this part of my story – which
was difficult enough to admit to myself, let alone
put into a song to share with the world.

I was taken back to the moment Elton first got in
touch with me when I was young, when I was at my
weakest physically. He was one of the very first to
reach out to me when I was diagnosed with cancer
at 18. He sent a beautiful big orchid to the hospital
while I was there and then called me when I got
home from my first chemotherapy treatment
(although he had no idea what incredible timing he
had that day). I was lying back in Dad's big old leather
reclining chair, feeling like I'd been hit by a bus,
when he rang. 'Hello, Delta, it's Elton John here,'
he said gently. 'I wanted to say, on behalf of the
United Kingdom, we're all thinking of you.' I'd been
spending a lot of time in the UK before my diagnosis
and my album was No. 2 behind Beyoncé in Britain
that week but I obviously couldn't get back there
during treatment. So Elton and I had a lovely chat
and formed a beautiful connection over the phone.

Fast-forward a couple of years and I was back in the
UK for the Royal Variety Show. It's a big showcase of
talent for the royal family and Elton was performing
that night too, so we finally had the chance to meet
face to face. I went back to his room afterwards, along
with a few other people, and he again expressed to me
this sense of connection he felt between us and told
me how much he believed in my music and my voice.
He was so kind to me and just wanted to make sure
I was doing alright.

'Elton John and his music had a deep and profound impact on who I am today'

That same night, someone else in the room asked me if I thought the guy I was seeing was really right for me – and in the time that followed, I made some choices that completely changed the trajectory of my career in the UK. My life over there became tabloid fodder. It seemed like I was on front covers everywhere I looked – and for all the wrong reasons. All the focus was on my private life and none on my music, and it did put me off course there for a little while.

When I circled back around to these moments while I was making *Bridge Over Troubled Dreams,* I checked in with myself and reflected on that time and being in the UK, and it got me thinking, as the lyrics say, '*Have I let you down, Rocket Man?*' Getting into the wrong relationship is something almost everyone can relate to and there's no shame in it – we've all been there. But the choices I made at that time saw me run away from a scenario that could've been incredible for my career. I was only 20, 21 – still a kid, really – and I learnt the hard way that you have to be so careful about the decisions you make.

I was also dealing with a lot at the time – my parents were going through a divorce, I'd just finished chemotherapy – and while I definitely make no excuses, because all of my choices were 100 per cent my own, I can't help but think that being with a guy who wasn't right for me at that time had an effect on my career.

I learnt so much in that era but for a long time had this niggling doubt that I perhaps didn't do as well in my own space as I could've. Of course, I know now that I did the best I could at the time. But after looking back, I wanted to impart this to people: never let an opportunity pass you by. I know we are all discovering ourselves along the way but sometimes you know deep down when things aren't right and it's important to listen to that intuition. I wouldn't change my story and I don't feel any regret, because I love my life; it's more a reflection on what I learnt in that chapter and the things I associate with Elton John: a deep passion and connection to the piano and to music.

I emailed Elton recently, after I'd written the song, though we hadn't spoken much over the years. I told him about my life, everything that had transpired since we'd last been in touch and he sent me

an overwhelmingly beautiful message back that I will treasure forever. Seeing the whole world fall in love with Elton and his music all over again when *Rocketman* was released made me so happy and I just wanted to thank him for all he did for me, both as a person and as an artist.

Elton's kindness and his belief in my music have stayed with me over the years but I don't think that I fully understood the weight of those early moments with him until much later in life. I've always had this deeply inspired connection to him and his music, the way he plays the piano and the artistry in his songs and lyrical style. In those early days, I don't think I understood how to find within myself the artist that he knew I could

be. But I'm now proud of who I am and my experiences, and I feel as though I've come into my own. As the second verse says, '*I guess that I've finally arrived now, feel like I am truly my own self.*' So *Dear Elton* is also me acknowledging that I did eventually look in the right direction. In many ways, when I ask, 'Have I let you down?', I'm really questioning myself. But at its heart, it is an empowered, emphatic, dramatic song that helped me heal. I've shut that door on that now thanks to this song. I finally forgave myself.

'When I listen back to "Dear Elton" it sends shivers through me... I don't think I've ever been so brutal to myself in a song'

BEHIND THE SCENES

'I'm not a fairweather
person. I like to go
deeper with people'

BILLIONAIRE

BILLIONAIRE

I didn't drink till I was 27
That day I went to numb the pain inside me
The emptiness was showing
The hate around me growing
I thought I had to bury my self-worth

The Boulevard of Broken Dreams was building
The whiskey kept on turning into wine
Some people started asking
Oh where was all this going?
Then tried to pull the wool over my eyes

I've always been a lady
And that always saved me
I had to see the other side

My mama said, 'Go marry rich, girl'
It'll take your problems all away
But I lead life with my heart
And the world's not always fair
I'm gonna make myself that billionaire

I've never been impressed with money or power
'Cause I thought I'd be the one to rule the world
So many men would tell me
It would be the gifts they gave me
But that just don't make them my Mr Right

My name is Delta lady
You can't try to change me
I'll give you many reasons why

My mama said, 'Go marry rich, girl'
It'll take your problems all away
But I lead life with my heart
And the world's not always fair
I'm gonna make myself that billionaire

He said, 'Baby, hold my hand'
I'm not your baby, understand
I'm gonna need a grown-ass man
Who takes me for who I am

My mama said, 'Go marry rich, girl'
It'll take your problems all away
But I lead life with my heart
Though the world's not always fair
I'm gonna make myself that billionaire

Shake that wannabe
You're only gonna end up lonely
He's no good you see
The real ones love unconditionally
You got to shake that wannabe
You're only gonna end up lonely

Billionaire is one of my favourite songs on the record. It's gritty, unfiltered girl power. There's a toughness to its femininity, like a Nancy Sinatra track, with the lyrical vibes of her father Frank Sinatra's *I Did It My Way.*

I've always made my own choices (for better or worse!) and I don't believe in relying on anyone else for money, for power or to define my worth. I make my own dreams come true. That's not how we always feel, though, and I think that's especially true for women. While we have a lot of autonomy over our lives, there does still seem to be this persistent underlying expectation in society that, when a girl hits a certain age, she should give up on her career or her aspirations and just 'marry rich'. There's this notion that someone will come along and save you, but *Billionaire* is shutting that idea down. We have to take control of our own lives.

It's definitely something I've felt, as have so many of my girlfriends, and I know we're not the only ones. I've had several conversations around this idea with different women over the years and many continue

'I look back at that chapter and I'm actually not quite sure that person was me some of the time! I had a lot of fun, but I was ready to come out the other side'

to feel that pressure to bow to society's expectations. But love isn't about money – for me, falling in love means being true to my heart.

Of course I've had support on my journey and I value it so much but I've never relied heavily on anyone else. I always knew my path and have been fairly headstrong in following my calling. But I did go through what I'd call my 'teenage years' in my late twenties! I was in Los Angeles, living it up, having fun, dating a few different guys... It was the first time I had really been single. I met some incredible people from so many different walks of life who had amazing insights about the world and I was lucky enough to experience some wonderful moments. I had so much fun! But that time was also admittedly a bit of a reaction to backlash I was receiving back home in Australia. I was caught up in the early wave of social media bullying and needed to take a time out from all the proverbial rocks being thrown at me. It's hard to deal with that kind of hatred being projected onto you due to other people's

> 'There is so much pressure on women to look to a partner to lift them up... But we can own our own hearts, our own homes, and we can be our own bosses'

misinformed ideas and I needed to take a minute. With that said, though, I would not be me if I hadn't gone through that chapter. I'm glad I have those stories to tell my grandkids one day!

It was around this time that an acquaintance suggested I 'just go marry rich'. (It wasn't actually my mum, like the lyric says – I took a bit of artistic licence there. Sorry, Mum!). But that concept didn't sit right with me. I was at this point where I had lost a lot, but those words reawakened my fiery side and I thought, 'That is not me. That's not how I roll. That is not who I am.'

So as that crazy roller-coaster ride began to slow down, I came back to Australia. This guy who was keen on me flew out here to see me, hired a boat and took me out for the day, hoping to woo me – he was such a sweet and fantastic person. Nothing romantic ever happened between us, as I'd realised that I didn't want a boyfriend at that point in my life – I wanted to commit to myself – but some of our incredibly deep, insightful conversations about life have stayed with me.

He was a champion in his field and he said to me one night, 'Delta, people aren't interested in how I win when I win – they're interested in how I come back after I lose.' I remember sitting on a swing with this wonderful human on a buzzing, balmy summer evening, watching the lights twinkle on the water in

Sydney's stunning Vaucluse – and even though we were really just ships passing in the night for each other, that beautiful moment touched my soul.

As I was finally ready to leave that chapter and get back to making music, he said to me, 'It's all about what you do next; it's how you come back. That's what people want to see because it's what they want to know for themselves. How do you come back? How did you overcome this?' That conversation was such a turning point and a fitting end to that chapter of my life. I knew at that moment what to do: I needed to leave that scene and come back to myself. And it's exactly what I did. I put my head down, worked hard and had a No. 1 single and No. 1 album that year with *Wings* and *Wings of the Wild*.

I've always been very determined to support myself and have the freedom to fall in love with someone for their heart and soul, not for money or power. I'm a woman who can pay for herself and that can shift the power dynamic in a relationship, so it's also always been important to me to find a partner who can understand and be supportive of my career. I was never really impressed by money or status; I've always been about heart and soul, and this song is about flipping social constructs on their head and saying, 'I'm going to stand on my own two feet. I'm going to make myself the billionaire. Watch me!'

PARALYZED

PARALYZED

Doctor paused this life
He told me you won't fly
Cancel everything
You need some time to heal
And it may take a year
Reset the clocks again

Is this the way life goes?

Everyone is singing their love songs
But I can't seem find my own tune
I've been on the inside for so long
If they knew the truth
All of my plans have been silenced overnight
All that I know is paralyzed

To learn to speak again
Amongst the frustration
How do I begin
See I will find my voice
Rebirth is the only choice
Can someone lend me a little patience?

It's just the way life goes

Everyone is singing their love songs
But I can't seem to find my own tune
I've been on the inside for so long
If they knew the truth
All of my plans have been silenced overnight
All that I know is paralyzed
Is paralyzed

Is this the way that life goes?
It's just the way that life goes

With a little time
With a little hope
With a little light
You'll never know
For a little space
For a lot of love
Close your eyes and think of
A better time and big dreams
Open your mind for you to find
A little strength inside
Stop and rewind
Just stop and rewind
Stop and rewind

With a little strength inside
Stop and rewind

Everyone is singing this love song
And I feel like I have found my own tune
I was on the inside for so long
And now they know the truth
All of my plans they were silenced overnight
All that I know was paralyzed
Paralyzed

Everyone is singing their love songs
But I can't seem to find my own tune
I've been on the inside for so long
If they knew the truth

With a little time
With a little hope
With a little light
You'll never know
A little strength inside
Stop and rewind

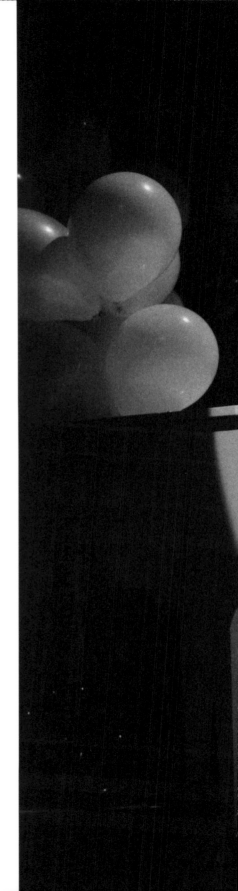

After learning how to speak again following the nerve paralysis in my tongue, I wrote so many versions of this song searching for the one that felt right – and when I played that opening melody on the piano, I knew it was The One. Every time I hear it, I really feel into every moment of that chapter, from the doctors explaining what had happened to the nerve, to speech therapy sessions in the hospital, to hiding out in Dural, north of Sydney, as I learnt to talk and interact again. When I sing *Paralyzed*, I feel as if I am watching the world, rather than in it; like I'm sitting still and everything else is moving around me. And that's how I felt while I was in the middle of this healing: like everything was moving forward and I had come to a standstill. I'd been meant to travel to London and had to quickly cancel that – all my plans had to be put on hold as everything became about getting well. All I could do was surrender and open myself up to possibilities.

I truly did see this chapter as a rebirth. It was a time to sit back, watch the world and create. As I worked my way through my recovery, I felt as if I was shedding pieces of my old self, uncovering a new me. Not being able to communicate fully and struggling to sing was such a strange experience; so I became an observer, taking in everything from the way humans interact with each other and the world, to how people reacted to me when I did speak. There were, of course, frustrating points but I worked constantly to keep my inner peace. Matt and I would sit for hours and talk about life; we'd go out for coffee, we'd get into nature, and that part was beautiful. There is serenity in letting go when you can't control a situation. The second you start fighting against what is happening, that peace begins to shatter.

I also felt a lot of gratitude because I have so much love in my life. I have amazing friends, a great little community of diehard loves. I run with ride-or-dies and in that chapter they were riding with me, without a doubt. We were just riding through it together.

'The reset is so important. I had to completely embrace it; to stop and rewind'

84

Of all the bridges I've ever written, the bridge in *Paralyzed* is one of my favourites. It's a real turning point, both in the song and my journey. '*With a little time, with a little hope, with a little light, you'll never know. For a little space, for a lot of love, close your eyes and think of... A better time, big dreams, open your mind, for you to find, a little strength in time, stop and rewind, stop and rewind.*' That bridge is so powerful to me because it gets to the heart of facing down hard times. I focused on the future, I imagined the fun and joy to come, I gave myself space to heal. Then, as that final chorus kicks in and the line changes to, '*Everyone is singing this love song and I think that I found my own tune*', it really completes the story arc. This track says exactly what I wanted to say and it's pretty special for me to have a song that is a real window into that chapter of my life.

I've had other health challenges in the past and as I spent some time reflecting on that before writing this record, I noted that my cancer battle at 18 was an incredibly different experience. Losing the ability to speak and to sing – which also meant facing the potential loss of my livelihood – seemed a much more private challenge and while I desperately wanted to find somebody who had gone through something similar to connect with, it wasn't something that a lot of people had shared online. I realised that, when I had Hodgkin's, I wasn't searching for other people to connect with; this time around I really longed for that connection and it just wasn't available.

'I love the metaphor in the line, "Everybody's singing this love song and I can't seem to find my own tune" – I needed to find a new way of being in the world'

I'd said over and over, 'I'm sure I'm going through this for a reason. I don't know what it is, but there has to be a reason.' Then, when I released the track and the video explaining exactly what had happened, people began approaching me with their own stories of communication disabilities. 'My mum had a stroke and she's not speaking properly at the moment,' one told me. 'She doesn't want to go out and when she speaks, people think she's drunk...' Having been through it, I understood. It can be isolating and jarring to see others' reactions when you're unable to communicate verbally. I couldn't even order a latte without the barista looking taken aback and that was confronting. I felt very disconnected... and my whole world is about connecting.

I had this incredibly powerful moment when I was back in LA. I was in a Starbucks and as the gentleman ahead of me ordered, it was clear he had some sort of speech or communication difficulties. The server was giving him so much attitude and it made me very angry. It was clear to me what he was ordering so I stepped in and said, 'He said a latte! Is that right?', turning to the man. He nodded and I just thought, 'Why was that so difficult? Did the server have to be so rude and impatient?' I had a very visceral reaction to that situation.

People sometimes forget, I think, to lead with love. They are scared of what they don't understand but if we all move towards the unknown with kindness instead of putting up walls, we can create space for compassion and inclusiveness. I don't have all the answers but I do know that the world could do with a little more understanding in moments like these. We love to talk about our individuality and uniqueness, so let's action that and celebrate it. This is not the time for fear.

'When you're forced to be quiet, you begin to listen more closely'

ALL OF MY FRIENDS

ALL OF MY FRIENDS

I couldn't sleep last night
And every time I tried
I saw the faces I was missing

Been chasing dreams since I was
17 and now I'm
34 and I'm admitting

That nobody knows me here
Another reason it turns into years
I know I'm fine here all on my own
But all of my friends are back home

My parents are getting older
They're always one step closer
There'll be a day they're not okay

My brother's having babies
I haven't seen them lately
I'm always just one flight away

So nobody knows me here
Another reason it turns into years
I know I'm fine here all on my own
But all of my friends are back home

Isn't it amazing how this works?
You spend your whole life building a world
You're always in a moment
This fight feels lost

And all of my doubt
Comes creeping out

Nobody knows me here
Another reason it turns into years
See I know I'm fine here all on my own
But all of my friends, they understand
But all of my friends are back home

Even though Australia will always be home, I obviously spend a lot of time overseas as well and was based in LA while I was writing this record. I do try to make it back home as often as I can because I love Australia so much, but I definitely do have those homesick moments when I'm away – and that was the headspace I found myself in when I wrote *All Of My Friends*.

I absolutely adore my life in LA but that intense longing for home hit me hard one day as I sat down at the piano. I was thinking about my friends and family

'The tears were rolling down my face as I sat down at the piano to play that day...'

back home, what they've been up to, how much I was missing and I ended up getting quite teary. I've been on the road, working as an artist for so long – all my life, really – and while I wouldn't swap this journey for anything, my heart was aching for Australia as I began to play.

It was a bit out of the ordinary for me, I have to admit. I'm usually pretty good on my own and I'm just as happy getting on with things by myself as I am when I'm surrounded by other people. But for whatever reason, on that particular day, I was feeling really disconnected from the friends and family I care

for so, so deeply. Of course, I have some of the most amazing friends in LA, too, but the tears were rolling down my face as I called Matt – who was also back in Australia at the time – and just sobbed: 'I really miss everybody!'

My family especially had been on my mind a lot. My parents are getting older; my brother's having children who I don't get to see nearly as often as I'd like; and as I was sitting in this moment of contemplation, awash with emotion, I was swept up in my yearning for home. The lyrics speak for themselves: I knew rationally that I was okay flying

solo there in LA – I do it all the time and, as I said, I'm usually fine on my own little train, chugging along! But all of a sudden, I felt like I was worlds away.

When I dug a little deeper into that sense of longing and homesickness, questions began to come up for me around whether or not I'm on the right path, which became a common theme that is woven throughout quite a few of the songs on this record. It can be so hard to get that balance right in life – not only for me, of course, but for everyone – juggling work, play, friends, family, love…

I'm someone who is fiercely career focused. I've always been this way and that's no surprise to my loved ones – they know it's just how I'm wired. But it does make hitting that work-life balance difficult and occasionally I'll check in with myself and think, 'Is what I'm missing worth chasing dreams all the time?' I often wonder, for example, if I'm spending enough time with my

brother's kids. I'm completely obsessed with them but I don't spend as much time with them as I would like to because I choose to have this incredibly full work life. This kind of realisation can really bring you to your knees.

Finding a way to balance chasing your dreams with all of the other parts of life that are so vital can be tough. And while the people who are dearest to me would never ask anything else of me – they love that I am living life my way and that I have the drive to chase my dreams – I do have moments when I ask myself if I'm getting it right.

'When I love people, I love them dearly; I'm fiercely protective of the people I care about'

97

KILL THEM
WITH KINDNESS

KILL THEM
WITH KINDNESS

I believe in peace, I believe in us
I believe we can change the world
One act of love

I was driving my car
Looking out the window
Feeling like this day was beautiful
Then this guy walked right by
He flipped the bird to the sky
Said our world's a lie and I asked why

I guess it's all just how you see it
It's what you want to go believe in

I believe in peace, I believe in us
I believe we can change the world
With just one act of love
I don't care if this song's too much
It's just we've had enough
Let's put it behind us
Let's kill them with kindness

First in line, coffee time
I was still half asleep when
Got the news that life turned upside down
First instinct was to bite
I can't change this if I tried
It's about more than my own pride

And when you're feeling like they're judging
Keep dancing even if they're watching

I believe in peace, I believe in us
I believe we can change the world
With just one act of love
I don't care if this song's too much
It's just we've had enough
Let's put it behind us
Let's kill them with kindness

Never think that your time is better than
Anyone we're in this together in
Making sure this world's
A better place for everyone
Send out the love you want to receive
To people that you see in the streets
Take the chance to do something kind

I believe in peace, I believe in us
I believe we can change the world
With one act of love
I don't care if this song's too much
It's just we've had enough
Kind, let's kill them with kind, let's put it behind
Let's kill them with kindness
Let's put it behind, let's kill them with
Let's put it behind, let's kill them with kindness
Kindness, let's kill them with kindness

'Instead of giving out hate, offer your heart'

The name of this track really speaks for itself. So many people are going about their daily routines totally disconnected from the people around them – heads stuck in their phones, screens cutting them off from everybody else. They seem to be angry at every minor inconvenience and it's as if everyone is presumed guilty until proven innocent, rather than the other way around. I'm not sure if it's always been like that or if I've become more sensitive to it, but it often feels like people are so quick to jump to blame and hatred, and compassion gets completely bypassed. So many people forget that mistakes can happen, accidents can happen – and they're usually unintentional.

Being on the receiving end of that sort of negativity can be intense and extremely overwhelming – believe me, I know, I've been there! But when I was a kid my mum always used to say to me, 'Why don't you try to make them smile so that their day gets better instead of letting them make you grumpy?' When someone has nothing to offer but hate, give back love – kill them with kindness.

The most poignant example of this for me happened several years ago, around the time I released my last record, *Wings of the Wild*. I'd had an incredibly tough week filled with difficult conversations and felt like I was taking hits left, right and centre. My beautiful friend Renée could see that I needed a night off and surprised me with tickets to a Beyoncé concert.

I was so excited to have a night of dancing and girl power with my bestie. When we got to the show, we were out in the fresh air, feeling the music, moving and releasing that tension, having the most amazing time. I looked up to the stars scattered across the night sky and breathed this huge sigh of relief. I was grateful for my life and my friends; I was feeling calm and carefree, and I had this deep sense that everything was going to be okay.

I was dancing away, feeling great, but there was this guy dancing beside me who was getting into my personal space and jostling me a bit. So I politely asked if he could move over – to which he replied (with a lot of attitude) that there wasn't any room. I shrugged it off and kept dancing. He continued to bump into me but I honestly didn't care – I was getting my fearless female on, feeling empowered and having the best time out with my beautiful friend.

What I didn't know was that, as I was out there dancing like no-one was watching, this guy was snapping a selfie with me – and by the time I woke up the next day, I'd gone viral. I can definitely look back and laugh about the whole situation now but, at the time, it was pretty crushing. I was just a twenty-something out for a good night with my mate and the next morning, I woke up to thousands upon thousands of notifications about this pic that some comedian I'd never even heard of had posted, with the caption, 'I got the most unrhythmic white woman dancing next to me at the Jay and Bay [sic] concert...'

Now look, like I said, I don't care now. To him, it was a joke (albeit not one I found funny, given I've always been a bit self-conscious about my dancing – nothing hurts like someone commenting on something you're already sensitive about). But the online vitriol that his Twitter post sparked was *intense*. I couldn't figure out what I'd done to cop that kind of hate and, as much as I wish I could say that I didn't care, I really did at the time.

People's eagerness to jump on that bandwagon and express so much aggression shocked me, but I didn't want to meet the trolls with more anger or pump any more venom into the situation. That's just not me. I knew the best way to diffuse a scenario like that was to lift the mood, so I tweeted that infamous *Seinfeld* scene of Elaine's daggy dancing with the caption, 'Had a blast last night. Delta ♥' – and the second I hit 'post' it was as if all of the air came rushing out of the balloon. I watched the whole situation fizzle out almost instantly; it was fascinating.

As much as I did feel under attack that day, I'm so at peace with it now. In fact, I'm grateful, because it freed me from my insecurities. That tiny bit of fear I had left over from when I was little and thought I wasn't as good as the rest of the kids in my dance class? Totally gone. Now, I could dance in the middle of the street for hours and you could say anything, and I wouldn't care, because there's nothing that hasn't already been said. I'm never afraid to hear constructive criticism or to check in with myself, to watch a show back and see how I could have done something better – but I'm also not afraid to call out bullshit behaviour. I think I have a pretty good sense of where I can improve, but some people are just straight-up mean and that's when you have to come back. But come back with lightness; kill them with kindness.

One of the first things I ever said when I broke through was, if you're not going to say something nice, don't say anything at all – and, quite frankly, I've got better things to talk about than being mean! We always have a choice in how we respond to whatever's going on around us. Choose to be kind.

'Only light can drive out
the dark'

CRASH

CRASH

She said that she'll be back in 5
She went to get supplies
In the pouring rain with her baby bump
Slowed down at the traffic lights

The driver hit the brakes too late
My mama raised up, 20 feet up to my fate

I got faith in the front seat
And hope by my side
Asking for the angels
To listen to our cries
From that day it made me
Be a fighter all my life
I got faith in the front seat
And hope by my side

They couldn't find a beat inside
We were running out of time
The doctor said there's 12 weeks left
But today you'll both survive

The driver hit the brakes too late
And I was raised up, 20 feet up to my fate

I had faith in the front seat
And hope by my side
Asking for the angels
To listen to our cries
From that day it made me
Be a fighter all my life
I got faith in the front seat
And hope by my side

My dad was going out of his mind
There was nothing he could do
So he went and bought my mum a baby grand

To take away her pain, give her strength
But the music was a miracle for me instead

We had faith in the front seat
And hope by our side
Asking for the angels
To listen to our cries
This is how my life started
It set the light inside
I had faith in the front seat
And hope by my side
I thank God for the angels
They listened when we cried

For a very long time, I didn't feel like the story behind *Crash* was mine to tell – I always thought it was more my mum's than mine. But when I started recording the voice memos about my life's journey from the very beginning (which formed the basis for this record), I realised that it is my story as well and is, in fact, a crucial part of how I came to be the person I am today.

Crash tells the story of the start of my life. It's a moment that has been explained to me over the years in different ways by my parents but it's something they don't like to speak about often – it was an incredibly traumatic time for both of them.

In 1984, when my mum was almost seven months pregnant with me, she was involved in a serious car accident. As a result, I was born nearly two months premature.

'I came into this world fighting...'

The day of the crash, there was a storm raging. Mum was waiting at the traffic lights in the pouring rain and the car behind her was going too fast as they pulled up at the lights. The road was slick with rain and the driver didn't brake fast enough – the car ploughed into the back of my mum's, pushing her, us, directly into the oncoming traffic. My mum was seriously injured and, with me still inside, she was rushed to the hospital.

I still wasn't due for another 10 weeks, so I was obviously not quite ready for the world yet. But as my mum was rushed into surgery, I was brought into the world; and as she underwent multiple operations, I spent the first days of my own life in the hospital's Intensive Care Unit.

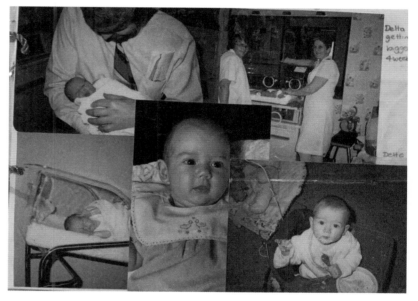

According to Mum and Dad, I looked more like a tiny frog than a baby when I was born. It was a very difficult time for both of us. Mum had multiple surgeries, both then and in the following years, including several jaw reconstructions. It was touch and go for us both and my mum and I barely even saw each other during that first little while. (Although one night, one of the beautiful ICU nurses smuggled me into Mum's room and put me onto her chest before sneaking me back out again.)

My poor dad was going out of his mind – there was nothing he could do but watch and wait and hope.

By some miracle – and with that fighter's spirit – both Mum and I lived to tell the tale. When we had recovered and were finally allowed to go home, Dad wanted to do something for Mum to give her strength, to commemorate that she'd made it through such a terrifying ordeal and to mark the beginning of our life together as a little family of three (my brother came later!). She'd always had aspirations to play the piano, so he went out and bought her one – and that baby grand was the first piano I would learn to play while I was growing up.

While there was nobody else in the car that day, I truly believe that we weren't alone. Something spiritual happened the moment Mum's car was pushed into the racing traffic. Like the song says, we had faith in the front seat and hope by our side.

The first moments of my life were unquestionably rocky for both myself and my mum. I came into the world literally fighting, which is a strange concept but a theme that seems to have found its way back to me again and again. I truly have been a fighter all my life. I've experienced a series of resets and sliding door moments over the years, which I've never taken for granted, and having that start to life gave me a deep connection to fate, faith and hope. Everything I've experienced along the way has taught me so much about myself, about kindness, about strength and tenacity.

As that final lyric says: '*I thank God for the angels, they listened when we cried.*'

'When I sing "Crash", it's as if I'm there,
watching the scenes play out in front of me'

PLAY

PLAY

Awake at 3am
I'm missing home again
Is this the life that I had planned?
Doesn't matter what I've done
Or how many things I've won
'Cause in the end I'd feel the same

When the lights go down
And they call last round
I hope I lived, I hope I loved
As much as I, I could have
Without rushing to the end
Stay true to who I am
I hope that I play

I hope that I play my favourite song
While dancing all night long
And laughed until I cried with my friends
'Cause when this story ends
It's easy to forget just how to play
So I'm just going to play

I'll play my symphony
Won't judge the melody
As long as it strikes a chord for me
My mum and dad, they told me
Regret will kill you slowly
Don't let it catch you in the end

When the lights go down
And they call last round
I hope I lived, I hope I loved
As much as I, I could have
Without rushing to the end
Stay true to who I am
I hope that I play

I hope that I play my favourite song
While dancing all night long
And laughed until I cried with my friends
'Cause when this story ends
It's easy to forget just how to play
So I'm just going to play, play, play

I hope I lived, I hope I loved
As much as I, I could have
Without rushing to the end
Stayed true to who I am
I hope that I played

I hope that I play my favourite song
While dancing all night long
And laughed until I cried with my friends
'Cause when this story ends
It's easy to forget just how to play
So I'm just going to play

In a way, *Play* is the song that really kicked off this entire record. Before we began working on the album, I gathered together a few of the people that I'd had some really special moments with musically throughout my life. Vince Pizzinga, with whom I've written a lot of songs over the years, and who worked with me on *Innocent Eyes*; Audius Mtawarira – we wrote *Born To Try* together; Anthony Egizii and David Musumeci, who I wrote *Wings* and some of my other hits with; and Matthew, of course.

So the six of us sat together on the couch and started talking about what kind of record I wanted to make and what I wanted to achieve with this new suite of music. We had a long, extensive, very deep conversation about all the ins and outs, and the sound and themes I wanted to explore. At one point, Anthony played me an amazing recording of author and philosopher Alan Watts talking about his take on the purpose of life and I was completely transfixed.

Life is like music, he said: inherently playful. You don't 'work' the piano; you 'play' the piano. 'One doesn't make the end of the composition the point of the composition. If that were so, the best conductors would be those who played fastest and there would be composers who wrote only finales!' The same goes for dancing – it's not about hitting that final pose, it's about the act of the dance itself and the emotion expressed within every single step.

If we think of life as being only about reaching the finale – whether that's a goal or the literal end of our being – we've missed the point, Watts said. 'We thought of life by analogy with a journey, with a pilgrimage, which had a serious purpose at the end, and the thing was to get to that end, success

'We shouldn't rush to get to the end of life; we need to play along the way'

or whatever it is, or maybe heaven after you're dead. But we missed the point the whole way along. It was a musical thing and you were supposed to sing or to dance while the music was being played.'

In both music and life, the point isn't to reach the destination but rather to make the most of the nuances, the highs and the lows; it's about doing our best to embrace every minute. It's something animals do instinctively – you don't tell a dog or a cat to play, they just do it because it's in their nature. It's something we need to embrace, too.

This whole idea – remarkable and quite beautiful in its simplicity – resonated deeply with me because I am inherently a very playful person. I work incredibly hard but at the end of the day I am that girl swinging from the chandeliers, dancing on tabletops, having a great time – and I would remind others to do exactly that. We are all, as humans, playful by nature. Don't get bogged down by the 'serious' stuff; don't deny the playful part of yourself.

The record starts with a single repeated note – a D – in *Keep Climbing*. *Play* closes the album and mirrors that opening, ending on a single note – a G this time. Between these two notes are the stories from the first part of my life, but it's only chapter one. There is still so much to do, so much to tell...

'We can all own our own stories
— this is me owning mine'

ALBUM CREDITS

1. *Keep Climbing* Written by Delta Goodrem, Matthew Copley, Sebastian Kole. Atled Music/Kobalt, Kobalt Songs Music Publishing (BMI); Coleridge Tillman Music/Universal Music Publishing (BMI); The Kennel AB Administered by Universal Music Publishing.
2. *Everyone's Famous* Written by Delta Goodrem, Marla Altschuler. Atled Music/Kobalt Songs Music Publishing (BMI), Kobalt Songs Music Publishing. **3. *Solid Gold*** Written by Delta Goodrem, Matthew Copley, Marla Altschuler. Atled Music/Kobalt Songs Music Publishing (BMI); The Kennel AB administered by Universal Music Publishing; Kobalt Songs Music Publishing. **4. *Dear Elton*** Written by Delta Goodrem, Marla Altschuler. Atled Music/Kobalt Songs Music Publishing (BMI); Kobalt Songs Music Publishing. **5. *Billionaire*** Written by Delta Goodrem, Matthew Copley, Marla Altschuler. Atled Music/Kobalt Songs Music Publishing (BMI); The Kennel AB administered by Universal Music Publishing; Kobalt Songs Music Publishing. **6. *Paralyzed*** Written by Delta Goodrem, Marla Altschuler. Atled Music/Kobalt Songs Music Publishing (BMI); Kobalt Songs Music Publishing. **7. *All Of My Friends*** Written by Delta Goodrem, Amy Wadge. Atled Music/Kobalt Songs Music Publishing (BMI); Cookie Jar Music LLP. All rights on behalf of Cookie Jar Music LLP administered by Warner Chappell Music Limited (ASCAP). **8. *Kill Them With Kindness*** Written by Delta Goodrem, Matthew Copley, Marla Altschuler. Atled Music/Kobalt Songs Music Publishing (BMI); The Kennel AB administered by Universal Music Publishing; Kobalt Songs Music Publishing. **9. *Crash*** Written by Delta Goodrem, Marla Altschuler. Atled Music/Kobalt Songs Music Publishing (BMI); Kobalt Songs Music Publishing. **10. *Play*** Written by Delta Goodrem, Matthew Copley, Anthony Egizii, David Musumeci, Vince Pizzinga, Audius Mtawarira. Atled Music/Kobalt Songs Music Publishing (BMI); The Kennel AB administered by Universal Music Publishing; EMI Music Publishing Australia Pty Ltd; Control; Blind Faith Entertainment Pty Ltd administered by Sony/ATV Music Publishing Australia Pty Ltd.